WEST

COAST

WILD

Text copyright © 2015 by Deborah Hodge
Illustrations copyright © 2015 by Karen Reczuch
Published in Canada and the USA in 2015 by Groundwood Books
Third printing 2016

Groundwood Books / House of Anansi Press
groundwoodbooks.com

We acknowledge for their financial support of our publishing program the
Canada Council for the Arts, the Ontario Arts Council and the Government
of Canada.

For Xavier, Molly, Finn and
Jack, with love. I look forward to
sharing many more west coast
adventures with you! — DH

To Rylan, who has waited long
enough. — KR

 Canada Council   Conseil des Arts
for the Arts   du Canada

 ONTARIO ARTS COUNCIL
CONSEIL DES ARTS DE L'ONTARIO
an Ontario government agency
un organisme du gouvernement de l'Ontario

With the participation of the Government of Canada
Avec la participation du gouvernement du Canada | Canadä

Library and Archives Canada Cataloguing in Publication
Hodge, Deborah, author
West Coast wild : a nature alphabet / written by Deborah Hodge ; illustrated
by Karen Reczuch.
Issued in print and electronic formats.
ISBN 978-1-55498-440-4 (bound).—ISBN 978-1-55498-441-1 (pdf)
1. English language—Alphabet—Juvenile literature. 2. Pacific
Rim National Park Reserve Region (B.C.)—Pictorial works—Juvenile
literature. 3. Alphabet books. I. Reczuch, Karen, illustrator II. Title.
PE1155.H63 2015   j421'.1   C2015-900036-X
C2015-900037-8

The illustrations were done in watercolor and color pencil.
Design by Michael Solomon
Printed and bound in Malaysia

 MIX
Paper from
responsible sources
FSC® C012700
www.fsc.org

WEST
COAST
WILD

A Nature Alphabet

DEBORAH HODGE

PICTURES BY

KAREN RECZUCH

GROUNDWOOD BOOKS
HOUSE OF ANANSI PRESS
TORONTO BERKELEY

There is a wild and beautiful place where an
ancient rainforest meets the ocean, where
whales swim and eagles soar. Waves splash
up on a windswept beach, and sea and sky go
on forever.

   Would you like to visit this special place?
Come and explore the Pacific west coast!
Discover some treasures of land and sea by
turning the pages of this ABC.

A is for an ancient forest that towers over a long sandy beach. Heavy rain falls in this rainforest and turns the trees into giants. Some are eight hundred years old.

B is for bears that den in the rainforest. At low tide, a hungry black bear ambles down to the beach and flips over rocks to find tasty crabs to eat.

C is for cougars that prowl at dusk and dawn. In the dim light, a big cat pads silently across the sand, hunting for raccoons, deer, seals and other prey.

D is for Dungeness crabs that scurry along the ocean floor. As a crab grows, it sheds its shell and forms a bigger one. Beachcombers often spot the old shells.

E is for eagles that soar overhead. Bald eagles nest in the tall trees of the ancient rainforest. Soon these eaglets will grow longer feathers and learn how to fly.

F is for fish that glide through the cool ocean. Eagles, bears and orcas feast on salmon, a fish that is prized by many west coast animals.

G is for gray whales that swim a long way. Every spring, these gentle giants travel from the warm waters of Mexico to lush feeding grounds in the Arctic.

H is for huckleberries that brighten up the rainforest. Sweet red berries are a summer treat for bears and birds. They gobble up these forest fruits.

I is for invertebrates that live in the sand and sea. The ochre sea star is an invertebrate — an animal without a backbone.

J is for jellies that shimmer and shift in the ocean currents. If they are jostled, these graceful creatures will glow in the dark.

K is for kelp that washes up on shore.
Thick kelp forests grow underwater,
providing a home for many young fish and
other sea life.

L is for limpets that cling to the rocks. Each small snail has a pointy shell and a strong "foot" that grabs on tight. Sea stars and birds devour them.

M is for marbled murrelets that nest in
the mossy branches of a tall rainforest tree.
Every day, the parent birds fly to the ocean to
catch fish for their baby.

N is for newborn, a black-tailed deer
seeing its first spring. A fawn's spotted coat
blends in with the light and shadows of the
forest and helps the new baby hide.

O is for orcas that leap and dive in the west coast waves. Orcas travel together in family groups called pods. Watch the young whales play!

P is for Pacific Ocean, the biggest ocean in the world. Its waters teem with life! Listen to the roar of the great waves. Feel the mist on your face.

Q is for quillback rockfish that swim near rocky reefs and live up to a hundred years. These fish have sharp quills for stinging seals and other enemies.

R is for rain that showers the coast and gives life to the forest and all of its creatures. More than ten feet (three meters) of rain falls in a year!

S is for sandpipers that flock on the beach. Every spring, these tiny birds rest and feed on the mudflats before they fly north to have their babies.

T is for tides that rise and fall endlessly.
At high tide, water washes over the sand. At
low tide, beachcombers find tide pools full of
colorful sea anemones.

U is for urchins that creep along the rocky ocean floor. A sea urchin has a spiky body like a porcupine. Sea urchins are a favorite sea otter snack.

V is for Velella velella, or by-the-wind sailors, that drift in the waves. Like little blue sailboats, they float on the water and catch the wind with their sails.

W is for wolves that swim in the ocean
and roam in the rainforest. Coastal wolves
fish for salmon, dig for clams and eat mussels
and barnacles on the beach.

X is for Xiphister, a prickleback fish that swishes through tide pools and hides under rocks. This fish breathes air.

Y is for yellow, the color of the sun on a hot summer day. The bright sun shines down on the coast, giving light and warmth to all living things.

Z is for zone, the intertidal zone, where land and sea meet. Every day, tides ebb and flow across the zone, revealing more ocean treasures for you to discover!

ABOUT THE PACIFIC WEST COAST

The Pacific west coast is a breathtakingly beautiful expanse of North America. It stretches along the Pacific Ocean from Mexico to Alaska and has some of the most majestic scenery in the world.

On the west coast of Vancouver Island, in British Columbia, Canada, is the magnificent Pacific Rim region, including Clayoquot Sound and the Pacific Rim National Park Reserve. There stands a temperate rainforest with giant trees that are hundreds (and maybe thousands) of years old. The ancient forest rises above a long sandy beach on the vast open ocean. It is one of the rainiest places on earth.

This unique ecosystem is home to a rich and diverse wildlife population. On land, there are large mammals such as bears, cougars and wolves. In the ocean, there's an abundance of marine life — from the microscopic to the massive, including orcas and gray whales. Bald eagles nest in the rainforest trees and hunt for salmon that are born in rivers, then swim to the sea. All of the species rely on one another in an interconnected web of life.

Farther north, in the Haida Gwaii archipelago, and along the BC coast to the Alaska panhandle (in an area known as the Great Bear Rainforest), is a similarly vibrant ecosystem. To the south of the Pacific Rim region is the Pacific Northwest of the United States, with coastal areas of Washington, Oregon and Northern California that also share an ancient rainforest and marine ecology.

All along the Pacific Coast, conservationists are working hard to sustain these tracts of pristine wilderness. Clayoquot Sound in the Pacific Rim region has been named a UNESCO Biosphere Reserve, marking it as one of the world's most important environmental areas. Here, people of the Nuu-chah-nulth First Nations have lived as stewards of the land and sea for thousands of years. In their words, "Everything is one and all is connected."

The Pacific west coast is an awe-inspiring place, with an extraordinary community of living things and a rare, wild beauty that is vital to preserve.

For Further Exploration

Pacific Rim Region
Pacific Rim National Park Reserve
   www.pc.gc.ca/eng/pn-np/bc/pacificrim/index.aspx
Raincoast Education Society
   raincoasteducation.org

Great Bear Rainforest
Pacific Wild
   www.pacificwild.org

West Coast Aquariums
You can visit, online or in person, one of the many wonderful aquariums along the Pacific west coast.

Look for aquariums in Vancouver and Ucluelet, BC; Seattle, WA; Newport, OR; and San Francisco, Monterey Bay and Long Beach, CA.

Books
One Small Place by the Sea by Barbara Brenner, illustrated by Tom Leonard. HarperCollins, 2004.
Shells by Brian Cassie (National Audubon Society First Field Guides). Scholastic, 2000.
Star of the Sea: A Day in the Life of a Starfish by Janet Halfmann, illustrated by Joan Paley. Henry Holt, 2011.

Acknowledgments

I would like to express my sincere gratitude to the following people for their help in the creation of this book: Adrienne Mason, biologist, writer and research coordinator, Clayoquot Biosphere Trust, Tofino, BC, for her thorough review of the manuscript and art, and for providing answers to a myriad of questions about west coast creatures; Dr. John K. Ford, Adjunct Professor, Dept. of Zoology, UBC, and Head, Cetacean Research Program, Pacific Biological Station, Fisheries & Oceans Canada, Nanaimo, BC, for his helpful information on whales; Ann Dreolini, MLIS Manager of Information Services, and Mayu Ishida, library assistant, Vancouver Aquarium, Vancouver, BC, for their advice on aquariums and terminology of species; Karen Reczuch, for the lovely illustrations that bring this book to life; and the amazing Groundwood team: Sheila Barry, publisher, Nan Froman, editor, and Michael Solomon, art director, for their wonderful work and warm welcome. Thank you all! — DH

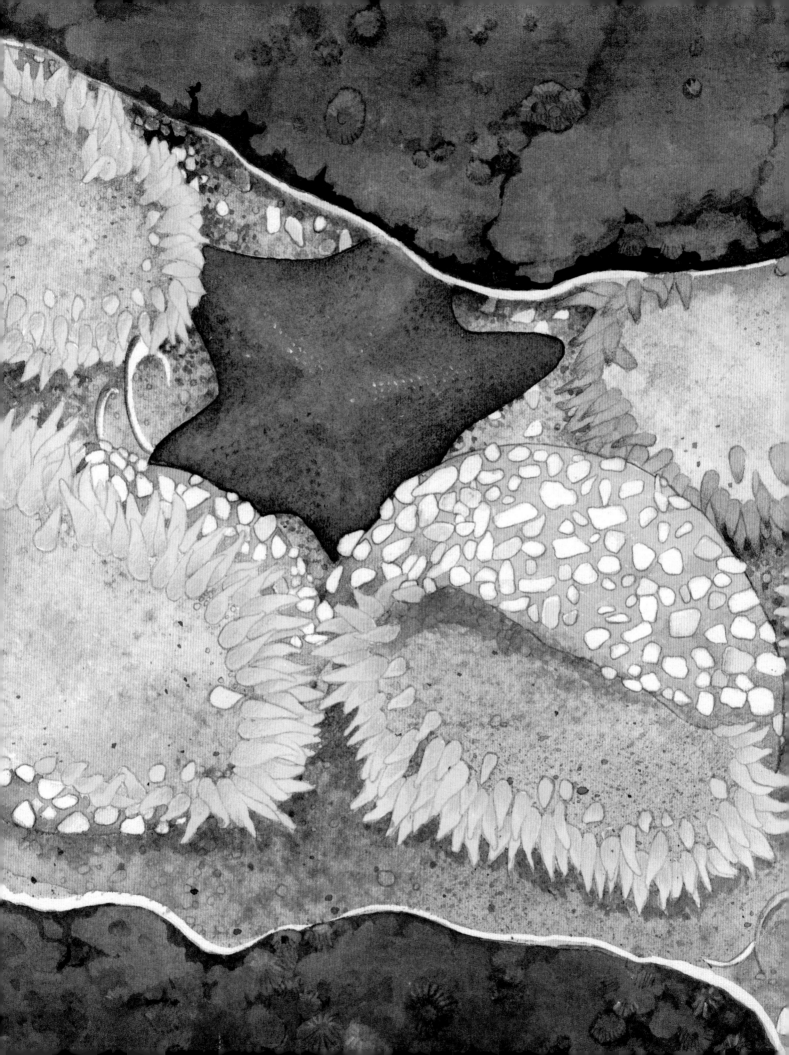